The Oxford Centre for Staff Development

Learning
in Teams

A Student Guide

994

1873576188

Graham Gibbs

© Oxford Centre for Staff Development 1994

First published 1993
Revised edition 1994
Revised edition 1998
Published by
THE OXFORD CENTRE FOR STAFF DEVELOPMENT
Oxford Brookes University
Gipsy Lane
Headington
Oxford
OX3 0BP

ISBN 1 873576 18 8 A Student Guide (Revised edition)

British Library Cataloguing-in-Publication Data. A catalogue record for this book is available from the British Library.

Designed and Typeset in 10.5 on 14 pt Palatino and Helvetica by Ann Trew
Illustrations from an original by R M Pomfret

Printed in Great Britain by
Oxonion Rewley Press Ltd
Oxford

Printed on paper produced from sustainable forests.

Introduction

This short manual is designed to be used by teams of students who have a project or learning activity to undertake together. Teamwork can be exciting and can involve the most memorable experiences of your course. It can also be frustrating and difficult. However, most of the difficulties can be anticipated, tackled and overcome. If you want to work effectively and enjoyably this manual can help. The manual contains advice, exercises and checklists you can work through in your team. If you have tackled teamwork before, these exercises will still be useful. Teamwork is a bit like time–management – it is a regular source of potential problems which will stay with you all your life, however good at it and however experienced you are. Yet a focus on what happens in the teams you belong to can lead to greater efficiency and more enjoyment as you progress. Every new team and every new task will call for a fresh approach. As you become more experienced you will recognise which aspects of your teamwork require attention and you will become better at making your team effective quickly and painlessly.

While you will gain something from simply reading this guide, you will gain a great deal more if everyone in your team reads the same section and you then discuss it. It will also help to do more than chat about the advice. Some of the sections have exercises associated with them so you can work through the ideas and advice together and come up with clear decisions about how to operate more effectively and enjoyably in the future. It is particularly important to do this right at the start, before you fall into unproductive patterns of working and behaving. If you are involved in a major piece of team project work and would like to really get to grips with learning about making your team effective, there is also a much longer book (*Learning in Teams: A Student Manual*) containing 27 structured exercises for teams to work through. Good luck!

Graham Gibbs

The manual contains the following ten pieces of advice:

A Student Guide

1 Be clear what the project is all about

Often at the start of a team project there is a sense of muddle and confusion about what you are doing and where you are going. While this is often a creative phase when many ideas are sorted out, it is vital that your team tries as soon as possible to gain a clear sense of exactly what is required in your project and that all members share the same understanding. Without this you will misdirect effort, pull in different directions and end up with poorer marks. Between you you need to have written answers to the checklist of questions below. If you can't answer the questions through discussion, or by referring to a project guide or course guide, then you need to go and find out and bring the answers back to the team. You may be able to ask your tutors, students from other teams or students from last year who went through the same exercise. You may be able to gain access to past project reports or even to an examiner's comments on all the project reports from the previous year.

What is the purpose of the project?
What are you supposed to learn? What skills are you supposed to develop? What earlier parts of the course does the project build on? What does it lead on to?

What are you supposed to produce?
What should the product look like? How big should it be? Is it like work you have produced before or does it have unique features? Are there examples of past project reports in the library or the departmental office?

What criteria will be used to assess it?
What will get good or poor marks? Which criteria are more important? What would an excellent product or a bare pass look like?

What are the main components of the project?
Are there clear stages to go through? Will the product consist of clearly defined elements?

What are the deadlines?
When is the final deadline for submission? What happens if you miss it? Are there intermediate deadlines for parts of the project? Are there optional dates for things like submission of draft reports or project presentations?

Are there project guidelines?
Is there a booklet or guide? Can your tutor brief you? Are there preferred approaches, topics or forms of report?

Are there hidden agendas?
Is it risky to be creative or unusual? Are there really preferred theories, approaches or methods even if it is supposed to be up to you to choose?

Are you supposed to do it on your own?
Will you be marked down for consulting tutors frequently? Can you work co-operatively with other teams?

How will it be assessed?
Do all the marks hang on a team report? How will marks be allocated to individuals within the team? What happens if there are disputes about team members who don't pull their weight?

And, finally, how will you get the answers to all these questions?
Perhaps you could each take responsibility for finding out about two of them and then report back to your team.

2 Be selective about who you work with

Team Size

The size of your team may have been fixed by your tutor. If you have a choice, bear the following things in mind:

- Small teams work faster and it is easier to manage and co-ordinate the work of the team members. If the project is relatively small and short in duration then go for a small team of three or four.

- A small team may lack a full range of expertise or team skills, including the creativity to produce good ideas, and can be vulnerable to one member dropping out, falling ill or not pulling their weight.

- Large teams, of six to eight, can cope with larger projects. They can generate more ideas, get more work done, allow the work to be shared out, collect and analyse more data, do more background reading and so on. They can also cover for missing or slack members.

- Large teams can be very difficult to organise and it can be particularly difficult to pull the work of a large team together and write a team report or give a team presentation. They need more structure, more formal meetings, clearer roles for each individual, and so on.

- Teams of eight and above are only for those with excellent team management skills and plenty of time to complete the task.

Team Membership

Selecting team members isn't just about getting together with friends. In fact teams of friends tend to work rather poorly together on projects because they may not feel able to be tough enough with each other – it can be too cosy, with no rigour or organisation. Neither is it simply a matter of choosing the brightest or those who get high marks. Bright students may be incompatible and very poor at co-operating with each other. Effective teams contain a balanced range of types of team member whose different strengths complement each other. For example, it is no good having a team full of creative people with no-one who is good at getting on with the leg-work. It can also be a disaster to have a team full of chiefs with no Indians. Use the checklist overleaf to help you to define your own strengths and preferences and those of your team members – it may show you that you have an unbalanced team, that you need to add someone to fill a crucial role, or that you are all trying to do the same job and leaving crucial jobs undone.

It may be that your team has been chosen for you by your tutor. You will still need to identify your strengths and preferences, and if they are unbalanced you will then need to decide who is going to play to their strengths and who is going to perform other crucial roles which would otherwise get missed out.

A Student Guide

Team Roles

Use this table to think about who in your team would best play which team roles.

Role	Who is like this?	Who is not like this?
Innovator Produces ideas, imaginative, unorthodox, radical, clever, uninhibited. Can be over-sensitive, prickly. May need careful handling.		
Investigator Finds things out, always knows someone who . . ., brings information back to the team, enthusiastic, gregarious. Can be lazy and complacent.		
Chairperson Self-confident, commands respect, good speaker, thinks positively, good at guiding the team. Can be domineering, bossy.		
Shaper Energetic, drives everyone along, needs to succeed, makes things happen. Can be disruptive and argumentative, impatient and a problem if things don't go their own way.		
Evaluator Careful, makes intelligent judgements, tests out ideas, evaluates proposals, helps the team avoid mistakes. Can become isolated and aloof, pessimistic or over-critical.		
Team worker Sympathetic, understanding, sensitive, shows a strong concern for social interaction, leads from behind. Places the team above personal concerns. May be indecisive		
Organiser Methodical, hard-working, reliable, orthodox, turns ideas into plans which are feasible and gets down to tasks which need doing. Can be inflexible and uninspiring.		
Finisher Painstaking, conscientious, follows through and works hard to finish things properly. Meets deadlines and pays attention to detail. Can be over-anxious and perfectionist.		

Based on Belbin, R.M. (1981) *Management Teams*. Heinemann.

3 Take the trouble to build a real team

Just because you have been lumped together in a cluster of six or so others doesn't make you a team. You have to work at becoming a team and the work you do at the start will be very important. If you just fall into getting on with some work you will probably run into all sorts of problems. How you behave when you are first together will have quite an impact on the team and how you behave for the rest of your time together. If you start off formal and quiet it may well stay like that for a long time. If you start off fast and enjoyably that, too, will stay with you.

So get it right!

What you can do to form a team

get to know each other

do something social together

do something risky together

carry out a task together

do something physical together

disclose personal information about yourself

express feelings about being in the team

identify your strengths and potential shortcomings as a team

identify your skills which may be useful to the team

identify your preferences about how you like to work with others

build, make, construct, draw something together

What you can do to avoid becoming a team

don't join in

have an aimless chat

allow an individual to dominate

allow members not to join in

keep it formal, neutral and abstract

avoid any expression of feelings

refuse to set yourself any task or goal

don't find out about each other

don't disclose anything about yourself

express criticism and hostility towards others

don't listen to each other

show no interest in the team

A Student Guide

4 Decide how you'd like it to be

There are implicit ground rules in every social situation: for example, about how polite you should be, whether it is OK to swear, whether personal questions can be asked, and so on. In a new team these ground rules are very fluid at the start – people will bring with them all sorts of assumptions about how things should be. It can be helpful to set up the ground rules that you want, and that will make your group pleasant to be in and an effective unit. Draw up your own list of ground rules and make sure that everyone gets a copy. Every so often go back to your list and see if you are keeping to it, or if you need new or different ground rules to make your team work well.

The following example illustrates the kinds of ground rules you might want to operate:

How we'd like it to be . . .

Sexist and racist remarks are not acceptable.

Decisions should be made democratically – if we can't agree there should be a vote.

Aggressive and dominating behaviour is not acceptable.

We should turn up to all meetings unless it has been agreed beforehand or unless there are unavoidable things such as illness.

Meetings will start five minutes after the agreed start time and everyone should be there by then.

Work should be shared around fairly and be seen to be shared fairly.

Tasks that people agree to undertake should be completed to the agreed deadline. If it looks as though there will be a problem meeting a deadline the person concerned should seek help from other members of the team in time to avoid a delay.

We should all try to encourage contributions from everyone – to discussions and to decisions – and to accept the value of everybody's contributions.

Roles such as chair of a meeting and note-taker should be clearly allocated and should rotate round the team so that responsibilities and leadership are shared.

Each person has the right to point out when these rules are being broken.

5 Make sure someone is doing it

If your team is going to be effective there are some crucial jobs that have to be done. If no-one does them then the team will drift aimlessly without achieving much. You need to decide who is going to do each of these jobs. Who does which need not be fixed for the whole team project. You may want to allocate them to the people who would like to do them or to the people who seem best qualified through past experience; or you may choose to take on unfamiliar jobs so as to learn how to do them. But whatever you do, make sure each of them is done by someone.

The most important jobs are:

Leader

A team needs a leader, or at least someone who will chair meetings. This person has the responsibility for clarifying the aims of a meeting, its agenda, for introducing each topic and for summarising discussions and decisions. It is the most difficult job to do well. It is possible to share this role in small teams or to take turns at it in larger teams.

Secretary or note-taker

A team needs someone to take notes in meetings, to keep a record of what has been decided, who is doing what, when the next meetings are and so on. If the note-taker isn't sure what has been decided then he or she should ask: "Before we go on to the next thing, can I be clear exactly what we have decided to do so my notes are accurate?" This person should produce an outline set of notes after the meeting for each member of the team.

Progress chaser

A team needs someone to chase progress – to see if everyone is doing what they are supposed to and that all the jobs that need doing by a particular time are on schedule. This person has work to do between meetings and should report on progress at the start of each meeting.

Time-keeper

In meetings the team will have a limited amount of time but a lot to do. Unless you are careful you will use up all your time on the first few things and not get the rest done. You will need to watch the time carefully and divide it up between your tasks. This is best handled by someone who asks: "How long should we allocate to this bit?" and then tells everyone when this time is up: "We've had our 15 minutes on this now." The leader, or the team as a whole, decides what to do next – the time-keeper's responsibility is simply to make sure everyone is aware of how long they have got and when this time has run out. It can also be useful to point out when time is nearly up so that the team speeds up: "We've had 15 of the 20 minutes we said we'd spend on this so we've only got five minutes left to sort it out."

> *A team of students had four members called Everybody, Somebody, Anybody and Nobody. There was an important job to be done. Everybody was sure that Somebody would do it. Anybody could have done it, but Nobody did it. Somebody got angry about that because it was Everybody's job. Everybody thought Anybody could do it but Nobody realised that Everybody wouldn't do it. It ended up that Everybody blamed Somebody when Nobody did what Anybody could have done.*

6 Divide the project up and share it out

A project can seem dauntingly large and it can be difficult to co-ordinate how you will get it all done between you. It can also be easy to suspect that you are doing more than your fair share or others less than their share. It is important to divide up the project so you can see exactly what needs doing, who is doing what, and whether the jobs are divided up fairly.

List all the jobs that need doing. This may be quite difficult at first and you are likely to need to come back to this list and add things to it as your project progresses. You may be able to get some help from last year's students. Be as specific as possible. Instead of writing down "Do background reading", you will need to list

what this might involve, for example: "Define the following terms: . . ." "Clarify the following concepts . . ." "Find and photocopy examples of similar studies in the literature", "Produce outline notes describing the methodology we will be using", "Find out what criticisms have been made of this methodology and what its alternatives are, and be prepared to explain these at the next meeting". Divide big jobs into their components and always be specific rather than general. Try to focus on the outcome of the job (e.g. an explanation to the team, a written handout or whatever) so as to make its purpose clear. Then estimate how long each job might take. Finally decide who does what. Write this down so everyone can see who is doing what and that the division is fair.

What needs doing?	How long it will take?	Who will do it?

7 Have proper meetings, not disorganised chats

Getting some work done in your team isn't the same as having a seminar or a chat. You may be used to tutors managing your meetings. You may be used to having no structure at all. In your team you will have to learn how to handle business meetings where work gets done. You need to be more structured than normal, more organised and more self-disciplined.

Formal meetings have an agenda, listing topics to be discussed, and notes are kept of decisions, for future reference. They normally have a chairperson to take the meeting through the agenda, opening and closing each item, summarising, clarifying and helping the meeting to reach decisions. The chairperson also has to

watch the time spent on each item, or has someone watch the time for them. There is normally a secretary to record decisions and the outcomes of discussion and to produce a summary afterwards for everybody – the minutes of the meeting.

Agendas help the group to make sure important points don't get missed and to divide time equitably between items.

They can take the following form:

- **Notes of the last meeting**: a list of who was present and missing and a record of what was discussed and decided, to remind everybody and allow everybody to check that they are correct; these notes should have identified who was responsible for doing what.

- **Matters arising from the last meeting**: what happened as a result of the decisions taken, what progress has been made on action.

- **Items for discussion**: these have usually been agreed beforehand, and form the core of the meeting.

- **Any other business (AOB)**: additional items which have arisen as a result of the discussions or which have been raised since the agenda was formed.

- **Time and place of the next meeting**: and a statement of what the meeting will be for.

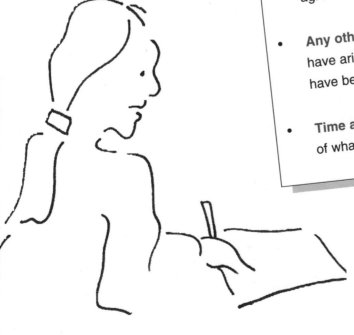

Try holding a more formal meeting, with an agenda and a chair and secretary, and then use the checklist overleaf to discuss how well it went and what you need to change to make future meetings better.

Whatever you do when you meet, make sure you sit so that everyone can see everyone else's face – preferably in a circle.

Meetings checklist

☐   It was clear who was taking responsibility for chairing the discussion.

☐   It was clear who was taking notes.

☐   We reviewed our last meeting.

☐   We reviewed our progress since the last meeting.

☐   Before we arrived it was clear what the meeting was meant to achieve.

☐   It became clear at each stage what the meeting was meant to be achieving.

☐   We had a clear list of things to discuss and work on.

☐   The business of the meeting was conducted briskly.

☐   We moved through the various topics in an orderly way.

☐   We spent a balanced amount of time on the different things we discussed.

☐   The discussions were focussed around decisions which we needed to make.

☐   We made clear decisions and recorded these.

☐   There will be a written summary of what we agreed.

☐   We have agreed a time and place for the next meeting.

☐   We know what the next meeting will be for.

☐   The meeting was effective.

☐   The meeting was enjoyable.

What else is going on in your meetings?

8 Discuss how it is going

All teams have problems and it isn't always easy to discuss them and sort them out. But if you don't tackle them they won't go away. The checklist below can help you to raise and discuss issues in your team. Go through it on your own first, ticking the items which describe what is happening in your team, and add one observation of your own. Then sit down with the others in your team and see if you have ticked the same things. Once you have accepted that you have some problems it is easier to discuss what to do about them.

What's going wrong in the team?

☐ We don't listen to each other.

☐ We keep repeating arguments instead of moving on.

☐ We constantly interrupt each other.

☐ We just push our own views instead of developing and encouraging others' ideas.

☐ We allow dominant members to dominate.

☐ Some of us don't contribute.

☐ We don't compromise enough.

☐ We concentrate on making impressions rather than on getting the jobs done.

☐ We don't have clear tasks or objectives.

☐ We are not clear about what has been decided.

☐ We don't make it clear who is to take action on decisions.

☐ We put each other down.

☐ We don't recognise that others have feelings about what is happening in the team.

What else is going wrong?

9 Give each other feedback – gently

Even if you have spotted and correctly diagnosed a problem in your team this doesn't mean that you have solved the problem. You will have to talk about it and decide what to do. And this may well involve telling others in the team about their behaviour and also receiving feedback from others about your behaviour. Giving and receiving feedback isn't often socially acceptable and when it is done badly it can produce strong emotional reactions which can cause more trouble than the problem the feedback was intended to solve. If you are going to influence the behaviour of others so that your team works more effectively you are going to have to learn to give and receive feedback sensitively and skilfully. If you follow the guidelines below you will find the giving and receiving of feedback less fraught and more effective. Start off gradually, giving positive, supportive feedback privately, in pairs with no-one else listening in – for example taking turns to say what you find helpful about another team member's work in the team, and move progressively to frank feedback during normal meetings, as in the steps outlined here:

- Try giving feedback in the safety and privacy of pairs. In pairs, take turns to give some positive feedback. Make a positive statement, saying what you like about the other person:

"Something I've noticed about you in the team is . . ."

- Then take turns to give some feedback intended to change the other person:

"Something I've noticed about you is . . . and it would help me if you . . ."

- This need only take a few minutes. Then come back together and discuss what it was like giving and receiving the feedback. Don't discuss the feedback itself: that is confidential to the pairs.

- Then take the riskier step of giving and receiving feedback in the whole team. Take turns to give some positive feedback to each person in the team: a positive statement, saying what you like about the others.

- Then take turns to give some feedback intended to change some aspect of each of the others.

- Finally, try giving feedback, positive and negative, in the course of ordinary meetings, but watch out for breaking the guidelines on page 11.

Guidelines for giving feedback

- Be descriptive rather than evaluative, for example: "You didn't bring the notes to the team which we agreed you would," rather than "You are lazy and unreliable." If you describe what you actually see and hear this reduces the need for the other person to react defensively.

- Reveal your own position or feelings, for example: "I felt intimidated when you argued your point," rather than "You were very aggressive." Describing your own reaction leaves the other person free to use this feedback or not as they see fit.

- Be specific rather than general, for example: "When you spent ten minutes trying to find your data I lost interest," rather than "You are disorganised."

- Give feedback about behaviour that your team members can control. It would not be helpful to comment on someone's lisp.

- Giving feedback is more effective when it is requested than when it is offered unsolicited. You can ask someone: "Would you like some feedback?" but if they say "no" then you shouldn't impose it.

- Check out the accuracy of your feedback with others in the team to see if they noticed and felt the same things.

- In general feedback is most useful at the earliest opportunity after the given behaviour.

- Check that you have communicated your feedback clearly. Ask the person to rephrase your feedback in order to see if it corresponds closely to what you intended.

Guidelines for receiving feedback

- Listen to the feedback. Try to understand the other person's feelings.

- Give the feedback serious consideration and weigh up the consequences of changing or not changing. Don't reject it immediately.

- Express your thoughts and feelings about the feedback and about possible changes in your behaviour, for example: "What you say feels about right, but if I tried what you are suggesting then I would probably feel . . . "

- Tell the person about whether you intend to try to change, and in what ways.

- Tell the person what they could do to help you to change, for example: "If you notice me getting like that again, can you give me a quiet nudge?"

- Express appreciation of their concern: say "Thank you for the feedback."

10 Plan your team presentation carefully

It isn't much use working well as a team throughout a project if you fall apart at the end and present the outcomes badly. You may be asked to give a team presentation and you may be judged, in part, on the extent to which this reporting is a team effort rather than the work of your best presenter or writer.

Presentations by individual students to a group are often boring. Presentations by a team to other teams are very often boring. The different bits aren't co-ordinated. They take too long. And the audience is made up of people who are more interested in their own team presentation than in yours. Unless you plan carefully it could be really dull. Use the checklist to help you to plan your team presentation.

You can use your team as a source of ideas and feedback if you practise beforehand. Other people, such as others in your team, are usually better placed to gauge how well you are coming across, so you can use them to help you spruce up your act.

How not to give a boring presentation . . .

1 Don't forget that there is an audience

A presentation does not only involve your speaking, it also involves your audience's listening. Why should your audience bother to listen to what you have to say? You have to interest them at the start and find ways of making them listen. Think about what might intrigue them, puzzle them, contradict their expectations, be controversial or entertaining. Think about what they already know and how they could relate that to what you have to offer. Think about your audience, not just about your material.

2 Don't include too much content

Inexperienced presenters almost always have too much material to present, and rush through it, overburdening their audience and still taking too long. Teams are even worse. 20 minutes uninterrupted listening is the limit on most people's concentration, even when the presentation is riveting. Cut down your content and slow down on your rate of presentation. Have a practice and time how long it takes. If you are worried about running out of material give yourself time-fillers such as extra examples, something for the audience to read, or questions for the audience to answer and discuss part-way through your presentation.

3 Say where you are going

It is difficult for an audience to listen to a team presentation for long if they don't know where they are going with your talk, or why. You need to explain, at the start, what the audience are in for and where you will take them. It isn't much help just saying: "Today is about X." You need to explain how you will tackle X and what you will spend time on. You may want to select one of your team to do all the introductory and linking bits. For example: "We've chosen three texts to analyse to illustrate our points, X, Y and Z. John will use the first two to show how . . . and Mary will use the third to contrast that with . . . After each text Bindi will summarise our points."

4 Let your audience know where you've got to

Team presentations can get complicated and hard to follow. The next person to speak can feel nervous and rush into their bit without explaining how it fits into the whole team presentation. Your audience will get lost if you don't give them a map of where you are going. It can be helpful to give some signposts along the way to show them where you have got to and where you will be going next. For example: "So Mike has looked at this first text and shown how . . . by giving examples of . . . and now June is going to . . . before Mary goes on to . . ."

5 Give the audience something to look at

It is hard just to listen to a team presentation. People find it easier when they have something to look at too. Provide your audience with handouts (containing a summary of your seminar, extracts from texts or crucial passages from your central sources). Use a whiteboard or blackboard to summarise your points or illustrate what you are talking about. Show flip-chart sheets, prepared beforehand, which provide an overview, a map, a diagram. Use an overhead projector and prepare transparencies on each of your main points. Give your audience something to look at while you are talking. Each member of your team might want to use a different medium to mark the stages and to keep interest levels high.

6 Give the audience something to do

Just listening to a presentation is dull. It is more interesting if the audience have something more active to do. This might involve reading a passage, analysing a text, solving a problem, suggesting alternative ways to interpret or analyse a passage or historical event, suggesting examples of a phenomenon and so on. From time to time, give your audience some work to do. Use members of your team to go among the audience to help them get going and to keep them at your tasks.

7 Don't make your audience take notes furiously.

People won't join in, or even think very much, if they are furiously taking notes. Provide a handout so that your audience can concentrate on what you have to say. Your handout can help to structure and link the contributions of the members of your team, too.

8 Invite questions

If you talk non-stop, especially if you avoid eye contact with your audience, they are unlikely to ask you questions, even if they have questions in their mind. You need to invite questions. You can do this by saying at the start: "Please stop us to ask questions or seek clarification." You can stop and invite questions: "Before Brian goes on, is there anything you'd like to ask or for him to clarify?" You can stop and look round, inviting interruptions with your body language. Leave plenty of time even though the silence may feel threatening – it takes time to formulate questions. If none of these work, stop and ask people to write down two questions they would really like answered, give them a minute, and then take each person in turn and get them to read out one of their questions. You can even plant questions or have members of your team sitting in the audience asking pre-planned questions.

9 Ask questions

Involve and challenge your audience by asking them questions. Prepare questions in advance. Don't ask "closed" questions, to which there is a right and wrong answer ("Who wrote . . . ?" "Did . . . write this before or after . . . ?"), but open questions which can start a discussion ("What might be the problems of this way of looking at things?" "Is this the only way of seeing this?" "What is your opinion on this?"). Members of your team can go into the audience and ask these questions to sub-groups to get a series of parallel short discussions going on.

10 Summarise

When you have finished, don't suddenly stop and say: "Well . . . that's it really." And don't just stop when the last person has finished their bit. You will need a separate conclusion or overview. Summarise what you have said and make clear what the key points were. Make sure your audience leave with a clear impression of what you discovered or what your views are. Each member of the team could say two sentences summarising their contribution.

11 Don't ignore what your audience already know

People think more if they can relate what you are saying to what they know. Find out at the start what people have read and what they are familiar with and adjust your presentation accordingly. There is nothing more boring than going over ground everyone is already familiar with – especially if other teams have tackled the same project – or dealing with something so outside everyone's experience that they can't relate to it.

12 Don't read out your notes in full

Inexperienced presenters write out their presentation in full and read it out word for word. This is very dull for the audience and it isn't much fun for the presenter either. Experienced presenters rely on much briefer notes which give them an overview and a way

of seeing very quickly what they are supposed to be talking about and what is coming next. Methods include:

- index cards which each contain one key idea or sub section of the presentation;

- a handout for the audience which the presenters use as a framework for the talk;

- transparencies which summarise the key points and which the presenters use to remind themselves;

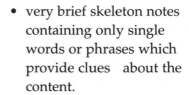

- very brief skeleton notes containing only single words or phrases which provide clues about the content.

You should aim to be able to look up at your audience most of the time, and to give the impression of thinking while you are talking.

13 Have some fun

Presentations don't have to be straight-faced and deadly serious. There will be more energy and involvement if people are enjoying themselves. Give yourself permission, and your audience permission, to relax and have a laugh.

14 Respond and be flexible

Things don't always work out the way you thought. If you are way over people's heads or boring them to tears by going too fast, don't just plod on regardless. You can have one member of your team watching the audience or sitting among them so that they can feed back to presenters what is going on and help to make decisions: "I'd skip the next bit – we are running behind time and they are getting bored," or "Mary will need to raise her voice a bit."